KIDS SPEAK OUT About

BULLYING

#PROTECT

MAKE A CHANGE!

Bully-Free Zone

#empower

SAY SOMETHING!

#KINDNESS

KIDS CARE!

BE A FRIEND

#SpeakUp

CHRIS SCHWAB

T0011536

Rourke
Educational Media

A Division of
Carson
Dellosa
Education

Before Reading: *Building Background Knowledge and Vocabulary*

Building background knowledge can help children process new information and build upon what they already know. Before reading a book, it is important to tap into what children already know about the topic. This will help them develop their vocabulary and increase their reading comprehension.

Questions and Activities to Build Background Knowledge:

1. Look at the front cover of the book and read the title. What do you think this book will be about?
2. What do you already know about this topic?
3. Take a book walk and skim the pages. Look at the table of contents, photographs, captions, and bold words. Did these text features give you any information or predictions about what you will read in this book?

Vocabulary: *Vocabulary Is Key to Reading Comprehension*

Use the following directions to prompt a conversation about each word.

- Read the vocabulary words.
- What comes to mind when you see each word?
- What do you think each word means?

> ### Vocabulary Words:
> - *alopecia*
> - *ambassadors*
> - *bystander*
> - *cyberbullying*
> - *disability*
> - *embarrassed*
> - *foundation*
> - *LGBTQ*

During Reading: *Reading for Meaning and Understanding*

To achieve deep comprehension of a book, children are encouraged to use close reading strategies. During reading, it is important to have children stop and make connections. These connections result in deeper analysis and understanding of a book.

 Close Reading a Text

During reading, have children stop and talk about the following:

- Any confusing parts
- Any unknown words
- Text to text, text to self, text to world connections
- The main idea in each chapter or heading

Encourage children to use context clues to determine the meaning of any unknown words. These strategies will help children learn to analyze the text more thoroughly as they read.

When you are finished reading this book, turn to the next-to-last page for **Text-Dependent Questions** and an **Extension Activity**.

Table of Contents

What Is Bullying?

Bullying is being mean to someone again and again. Sometimes, bullies call other kids names. They make fun of them. Bullies might take or break stuff. Sometimes, they hit, pinch, shove, or trip. Some kids get bullied on computers or phones. The good news is that kids can speak out about bullying and help change the world!

Bullying Happens Everywhere

Bullying happens too often. One in three kids around the world was bullied once or more last month.

Seventh-grader Natalie Hampton understood how it felt to be bullied. She sat by herself in the school cafeteria for an entire year. Once, a group of students pushed her down. Another time, someone came at her with scissors.

Natalie Hampton

Natalie knew she couldn't stop all bullying. But, she could help kids have a better lunch. She made a phone app called *Sit With Us*. The app helps kids find someone to sit with in the cafeteria.

The *Sit With Us* app helps student volunteers become **ambassadors**. Ambassadors make sure that all kids have someone to sit with at lunch. The app is free!

Part of the Sit With Us *app*

World Changing

In 2017, *People* magazine listed Natalie as one of the top 25 Women Changing the World for her anti-bullying work.

Different and Daring

Bullying is harmful. It makes kids feel afraid. It can make them feel **embarrassed** or lonely.

Many kids who are bullied say it is because of how they look or because they are "different." Being different can mean a lot of things. It can be about body size, race, religion, **disability**, identifying as **LGBTQ**, or anything else that makes someone stand out.

Ask for help if you or anyone you know is being bullied because of being different. Remember that everyone is unique. Everyone should be accepted as they are. Differences should be celebrated!

Sanah Jivani

Twelve-year-old Sanah Jivani was bullied in school. Kids made fun of her when she lost her hair. It came out in pieces. Soon, all of her hair was gone. She had a disorder called **alopecia**. There is no cure.

When kids at school bullied Sanah, she started to feel bad about herself. She bought wigs to cover her bald head. Then, she decided to love herself as she was. She stopped wearing wigs. But sometimes she wore a big ribbon around her head!

Sanah started a **foundation** called the Love Your Natural Self Foundation (LYNS). LYNS tries to help kids around the world. Sanah tells kids to be natural. She tells them to love themselves as they are. She wants everyone to feel good about themselves.

Sanah named February 13 the International Day of Self-Love. On this day, Sanah wants everyone to remember to be themselves!

Sanah Jivani shares her story at schools.

Getting Involved

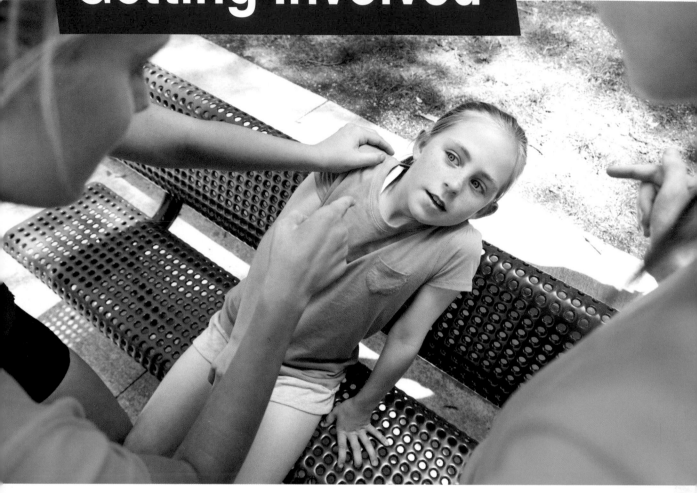

Together, kids can make a difference. There is power in numbers. You can work with other kids to fight bullying.

You can write an anti-bullying pledge. Pass it around your school. Ask your classmates to read and sign it. You can make a poster about what bullying is and how to stop it. Make copies. Hang them everywhere!

Then, when kids around you see someone being bullied, they will know what to do. Tell an adult. Call a friend. Make it stop.

Don't Stand By

A **bystander** stands by. A bystander sees bullying and does nothing to stop it. Instead be an upstander! An upstander stands up to a bully. An upstander gets help. An upstander is a superhero!

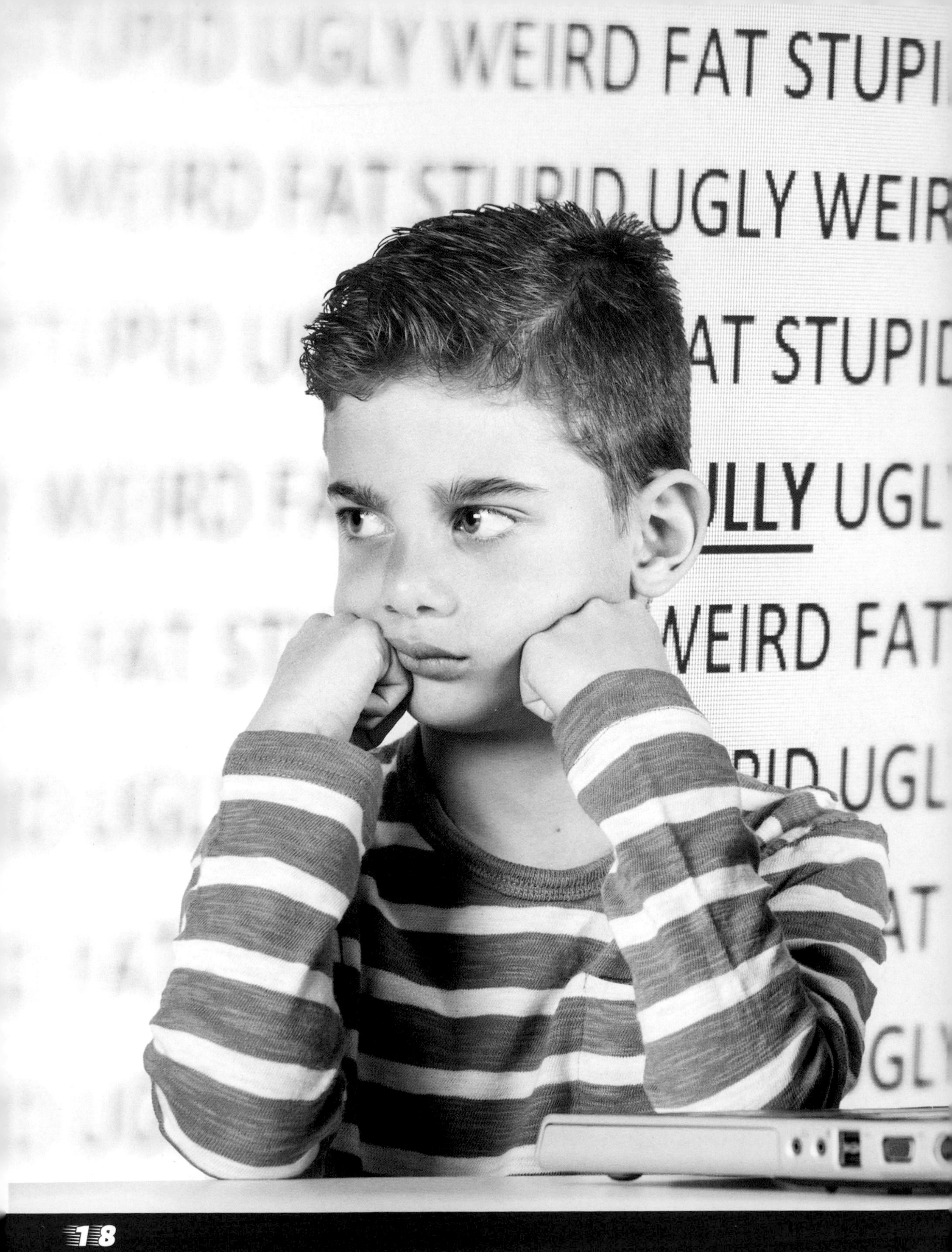
UGLY WEIRD FAT
UGLY
STUPID
WEIRD

Eighth-grader Matthew Kaplan took action against bullying. He noticed that his 10-year-old brother Josh was acting quiet. He wanted to be alone. Matthew knew something was wrong. Josh didn't want to open up. He got quieter. He smiled less.

Finally, Josh told Matthew that he was getting mean messages on his phone and on Facebook: "You're worthless." "What's wrong with you?" Matthew decided to do something about the **cyberbullying**.

Matthew Kaplan

THE BE ONE PROJECT

Matthew put together an anti-bullying program. He presented it to his brother's class. As the class got involved, the bullies apologized to Josh.

Matthew turned the anti-bullying program into a nonprofit company called the Be ONE Project. ONE stands for "Open to New Experiences." His project has been presented to thousands of kids. Matthew has starred in a Disney Channel commercial and has won many awards.

Just like Natalie, Sanah, and Matthew, you can speak out and help change the world!

Matthew presents the Be ONE Project to a group of middle schoolers.

CNN Hero!

CNN, a TV news channel, looks for "everyday people doing extraordinary things to change the world." Matthew Kaplan is a CNN Hero. He told CNN, "We want to create a culture where being inclusive and kind is the norm."

Top 10 Ways to Get Involved

1 Tell an adult (teacher, parent, counselor, police officer) if you see bullying.

2 Take the person being bullied to a safe place.

3 Tell the person being bullied that you feel bad. Be a friend.

4 Stand up to the bully. Have a friend or adult help.

5 Encourage the person being bullied to ask for help.

6 If someone is cyberbullied, help them set privacy settings.

7 When you hear nasty rumors or gossip, don't repeat them.

8 Don't cheer or laugh when someone is being bullied.

9 Eat with students who are bullied in the cafeteria.

10 Start an anti-bullying club at your school.

Glossary

alopecia (al-uh-PEE-shuh): loss of hair

ambassadors (am-BAS-uh-durs): the top people sent to represent a group or country

bystander (BYE-stan-dur): someone watching while something happens to someone else

cyberbullying (SYE-bur-BUL-ee-ing): posting mean-spirited messages electronically, often anonymously

disability (dis-uh-BIL-i-tee): a condition that limits a person's ability to do something

embarrassed (em-BAR-uhst): feeling ashamed or uncomfortable

foundation (foun-DAY-shuhn): an organization that supports a cause with money

LGBTQ (l-g-b-t-q): an abbreviation for lesbian, gay, bisexual, transgender, and queer or questioning

Index

Text-Dependent Questions

1. Name three ways someone might bully.
2. How could bullying make someone feel?
3. What is the difference between a bystander and an upstander?
4. Name one thing Natalie, Sanah, and Matthew have in common.
5. Name one thing you can do if you see someone being bullied.

Extension Activity

Many schools have an anti-bullying policy. Does yours? If so, ask for a copy. Read it with a group of friends or your class. Decide if your school's policy covers everything.

If your school does not have an anti-bullying policy, volunteer to write one. You could do this yourself, with friends, or with your class. You may want to ask your teacher to help. Then, take it to the principal. Explain why it is important.

About the Author

Chris Schwab is a writer and editor. She has written many articles for newspapers and magazines. Now she writes books for kids. She remembers what it feels like to be embarrassed in school. She used to teach special needs classes. Kids with special needs are often bullied. She hopes that someday no kid will ever be bullied for any reason.

Quote source: Kathleen Toner, "A brother's plight inspires an anti-bullying mission," CNN, October 14, 2016: https://www.cnn.com/2016/10/13/us/cnn-hero-matthew-kaplan-be-one-project/index.html

© 2021 Rourke Educational Media

All rights reserved. No part of this book may be reproduced or utilized in any form or by any means, electronic or mechanical including photocopying, recording, or by any information storage and retrieval system without permission in writing from the publisher.

www.rourkeeducationalmedia.com

PHOTO CREDIT: Cover, p1 ©ronniechua, ©Nikada, ©calvindexter, ©Hulinska_©Yevhenila, ©Bubushonok, ©ulimi; p4 ©Wavebreakmedia; p5 ©By Lopolo; p6 ©By Kathy Hutchins; p7 ©By wavebreakmedia; p8 ©PhoThoughts, ©Sit With Us app; p9 ©By wavebreakmedia; p10 ©kali9; p12 ©Pressmaster; p13 ©Svannah Nguyen; p14 ©monkeybusinessimages; p15 ©Boi-Han Nguyen; p16©SDI Productions; p17 ©By Rawpixel.com; p18 ©By Yiorgos GR, ©UT07; p20 ©Josh Kaplan, ©Sharon Berk, ©Cake Creative ©jasonfotos.com

Edited by: Hailey Scragg
Cover and interior layout by: Kathy Walsh and Morgan Burnside

Library of Congress PCN Data

Kids Speak Out About Bullying / Chris Schwab
(Kids Speak Out)
ISBN 978-1-73163-854-0 (hard cover)(alk. paper)
ISBN 978-1-73163-931-8 (soft cover)
ISBN 978-1-73164-008-6 (e-Book)
ISBN 978-1-73164-085-7 (ePub)
Library of Congress Control Number: 2020930267

Rourke Educational Media
Printed in the United States of America
01-1942011937